Contents:

C000243968

Acknowledgements:

This book is dedicated with gratitude to the original Quaker Tapestry teachers, Anne Wynn-Wilson, Ann Nichols, Ann Castle and Jill Robinson who set the standards and guidelines; created the energy and enthusiasm to continue; and gave their time and expertise with love.

My hope is that once you have completed a Quaker Tapestry sewing kit, you will be inspired to create your own designs in the unique Quaker Tapestry style.

Why not join us on one of the embroidery workshops at Kendal? The workshops are such fun and a fantastic way to bring like-minded individuals together to share ideas and learn new skills.

Happy sewing!
Bridget Guest

Bridget Guest

In the 1980s Bridget studied textiles, print, illustration, community art, photography and film within her Bachelor of Arts Degree in Art & Design followed by a Post Graduate Certificate in Education in Art/Design and Textiles. After teaching for several years in secondary education Bridget ran her own successful retail business. She began working with the Quaker Tapestry in 1994 and has been teaching the embroidery workshops since 1996.

Bridget has developed the embroidery course to encourage students in all aspects of the Quaker Tapestry embroidery techniques and design. The workshops are held at the Exhibition centre in Kendal and on request Bridget travels to other areas of the country to pass on her skills to other groups of people. Over the years the tapestry and the workshops have inspired other community groups to create their own textile projects, both small and large.

For more information about the Quaker Tapestry and the embroidery workshops visit the website: www.quaker-tapestry.co.uk

Introduction to the Quaker Tapestry

Anne Wynn-Wilson, the founder of the Quaker Tapestry

Anne Wynn-Wilson (1926-1998), the founder of the Quaker Tapestry, was an experienced embroiderer with enthusiasm for and a love of textiles. Her concern for the well being of the Quaker community led her to encourage and enable those who wished to take part in the creation of this unique community textile.

The creative embroidery and the lettering satisfied the experienced workers, whilst the simplified use of stitches made it possible to include children and those who had never undertaken any embroidery before.

At the heart of the tapestry scheme were the embroidery workshops. These still continue today at Kendal, and elsewhere when requested by groups, to share the Quaker Tapestry stitches, techniques and stories.

The workshops cater for both the absolute beginner and the experienced embroiderer, whether producing simple embroidery from a Quaker Tapestry kit or embarking on a large community project.

Anne wrote the first stitch manual for the Quaker Tapestry, 'Quakers in Stitches' (1995), now out of print. This was based on her original pamphlets, or guidelines for the project, from the 1980s.
This publication takes its inspiration from Anne's earlier book.

Bottom left to right:
Anne Wynn-Wilson in the 1980s.
Jonathan Stocks in the early 1980s.
A detail of children's work from panel C2 Margret Fell.

From the beginning of the project in 1981 it was Jonathan Stocks, a twelve year old boy, who suggested that embroidery should be used to tell the Quaker stories.

Narrative Crewel Embroidery

The 'crewel embroidery' technique,
just like the Bayeux Tapestry, is designed to
dance freely across the surface of the fabric.
There are no specific holes for the needle as
in canvas work, and there is no counting of
threads as in cross-stitch.

The word 'crewel' comes from the ancient word
describing the curl of the staple of the wool.
Crewel wool has a long staple, which is fine and
can be strongly twisted. Crewel embroidery
takes its name from this wool.

The distinctive style of the Quaker Tapestry depends on the use of six stitches and three layers of embroidery

The *first layer* of embroidery is the stem stitch
which follows the outline of the figure or
picture. Parts of this will remain untouched,
as in the face and hands of George Fox.

The *second layer* of embroidery provides the
plain area of colour and texture (shown in the
jacket of George Fox).

The *third layer* is the descriptive creative layer of
embellishment (shown in the shirt and hair of
this detail) where the stitches move freely over
both the plain shapes and the background fabric.

Detail of George Fox from panel E1
showing the three layers of embroidery.

Materials

A Quaker Tapestry sewing kit contains:

- Quaker Tapestry Woollen embroidery fabric 33cm x 33cm (13" x 13")
- Calico backing fabric, 33cm x 33cm (13" x 13")
- Embroidery needles
- Textile transfer pencil
- The 'cartoon' or line drawing
- Greaseproof paper
- Crewel embroidery thread
- 'Aqua pen' or water -erasable pen (only in the kits which include lettering)

Items of equipment needed:

- Sewing pins
- Paperclips
- Scissors
- An iron and ironing board
- Cotton tacking thread
- Embroidery hoop and stand or a seat frame
- Screwdriver
- Pencil and sharpener
- Ruler

If using this book with children please ensure adult supervision when using hot iron or sharp tools.

Needles:

With Crewel embroidery, we use a needle that is sharp and easy to thread.

Both 'Crewel Needles' and 'Chenille Needles' can be used with this embroidery.

A: Crewel Needles are sharp-pointed with large eyes, making them easy to thread.

B: Chenille Needles are also sharp-pointed but are thicker with larger eyes.

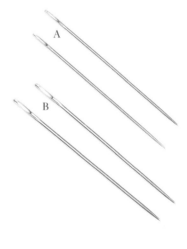

Fabric:

The Quaker Tapestry woollen cloth is a plain-weave fabric using a random warp that produces a low-key stripe. The stripe and the weave provide a guide to keep the line of the lettering and buildings vertical.

The woollen cloth is mounted on to a calico backing cloth, which carries the design for the embroidery and helps to stabilise the tension of the woollen fabric. The calico cloth will remain at the back of the woollen fabric and is not removed after the embroidery has been finished.

A woollen fabric was chosen for the Quaker Tapestry instead of using the traditional linen twill because it is more comfortable to work with and it doesn't show the needle marks if unpicking is needed

Threads:
The Quaker Tapestry uses 'Appleton's Crewel Wool' which is a fine 2-ply woollen thread.

The Transfer Technique

Transferring the design from 'cartoon' to woollen cloth:

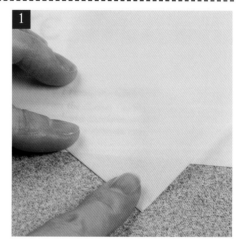

1. Find the centre of your greaseproof paper by folding it in half and then in half again.

Greaseproof paper is designed to withstand heat so is perfect for the transfer technique when used with a hot iron and a textile transfer pencil.

The design for the embroidery must first be transferred onto the calico or cotton cloth, which will later be attached to the woollen cloth.

A simple line drawing, or 'cartoon' is all you need, similar to those in children's colouring books.
The sewing kits provide a cartoon.

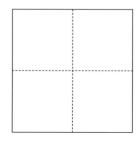

Example of fold lines to find the centre point.

2. Fold the cartoon in the same way as the greaseproof paper. Place the greaseproof paper over the cartoon matching the lines and fasten the sheets together with paperclips.

Using the textile transfer pencil

3. Trace the outline of the entire cartoon, including the lettering, using a sharp transfer pencil and the greaseproof paper. Use a ruler to draw guidelines at either side of the lettering.

Tip - to avoid smudging particles of wax from your hand on to your tracing, rest your hand on a piece of paper as you trace.

Transferring the design to the calico cloth

4. Find the centre of the calico cloth by folding it - as you did with the paper. Place the greaseproof paper, with the wax side down, on to the calico cloth matching centre lines - make sure the cloth and paper are flat. Hold them together with 4 pins.

It is important that the tracing is straight because the lettering needs to be in a straight line on the fabric.

Using an iron to transfer the design

5. Use a very hot, dry iron (no water or steam). The heat and pressure will transfer the design but do not slide or move the iron when it is in contact with the greaseproof paper. Make sure that all areas of the design have been pressed.

Tip - before you begin using the iron, protect your ironing board with an old clean tea towel.

6. Before removing the pins, make sure that the whole design has transferred to the calico by peeping underneath the greaseproof paper first.

On the calico you will notice that the design is a mirror image of the original - don't worry, that is how it should be.

7. Using a ruler and ordinary pencil, draw a line on to the calico at the top and bottom of the lettering using the guidelines.

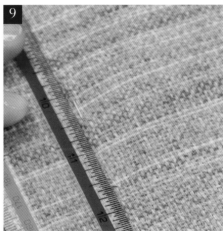

Sewing the calico and the woollen cloth together

Put the two fabrics together making sure that the strong lines (the warp) of the woollen cloth are vertical.

It doesn't matter which side of the woollen fabric you choose for the front, they are both nice!

8. To make sure that the design is straight, put pins through both fabrics at each side of the pencil line.

9. On the woollen side, place a ruler over the pins and check that they line up along one of the horizontal lines (the weft) of the fabric. If they don't line up, move the calico fabric and keep checking until the pins line up along the ruler.

10. Tack the two pieces together using cotton tacking thread around the edges of the design.

Example of tacking lines.

Dressing the hoop

1

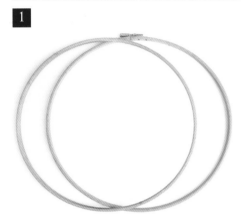

1. The embroidery hoop consists of two rings; the outer ring has a screw and is adjustable to allow for different types of fabric.

2

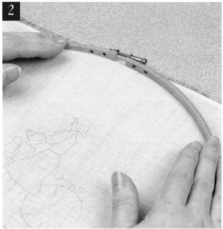

2. Place the inner ring on a flat surface or table; place the fabric with the calico side facing you, over the ring on the table. Slacken the screw of the outer ring enough to push the outer ring over the fabric and the inner ring, so that it holds the fabric firmly in place. The calico fabric should be taut.

3

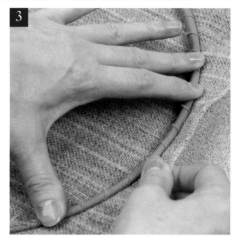

3. Turn the hoop over on the table so that the woollen fabric is uppermost. While holding the inner ring down with one hand, take just the woollen fabric and gently ease on the 'skirt' to remove any air bubbles.

Tip - Take care not to distort the weave of the woollen fabric.

Here are three different ways of holding the embroidery hoop. It is important to have both of your hands free to sew when working with a hoop.

a

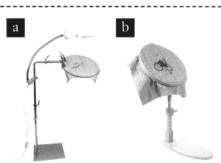

b

c

a. The embroidery stand, allows you to use a light and magnifier.

b. The seat frame allows you more freedom - it can be used anywhere.

c. If you don't have a stand use the edge of a table and a heavy book.

Start stitching

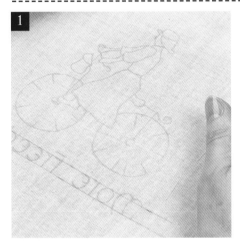

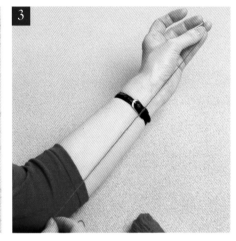

Preparing the fabric for working on the calico side first

1. Put the embroidery hoop in the stand with the calico side on top; work the outline of the cartoon in 'stem stitch' using the same colours as the finished embroidery. Do not outline the lettering.

Working with skeins of wool

2. First find the end of thread from the skein of wool that pulls easily from the skein.

There are two ends of thread within the skein of wool, one will be difficult to pull and the other will pull easily.

Tip - once you have found the correct end of thread to pull, leave this long so that you don't have to look for it again!

3. Using the correct colour of thread for the area you are outlining, cut a length which measures no longer than from your little finger to your elbow. Then thread your needle (page 16 & 17).

Threading the needle

If you have never used wool for embroidery before it is worth having a go at threading the needle this way. Wool is very different from cotton or silk because it's so hairy. You need to control the hairs when threading the needle and this method should help you. If you have never done this before you may find it tricky to begin with but keep practising....

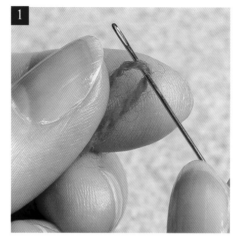

1. Loop the wool thread over the needle.

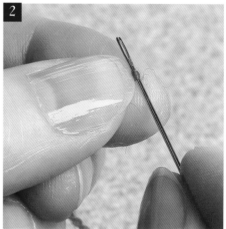

2. Pinch it between your first finger and your thumb.

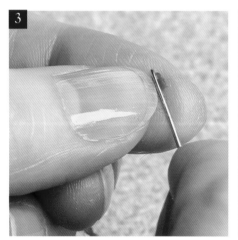

3. Pull the needle out then roll the eye of the needle over the wool.

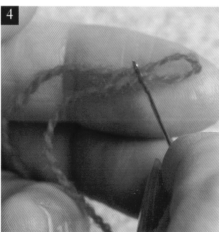

4. Pull the thread through the eye of the needle with your thumbnail.

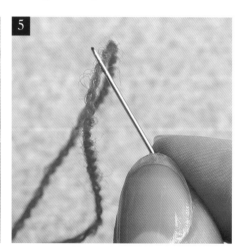

5. The threaded needle.

6. Tie a knot in the end of the thread furthest away from the needle; this will stop the thread pulling all the way through when you begin to sew.

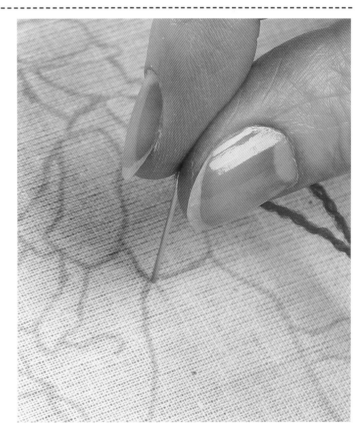

Stitching Technique

The 'stab' method of stitching, when using a hoop, is to hold your needle vertically, like a dart and go down completely through to the underside of the fabric and then turn the needle round and come back up again.

More Freedom

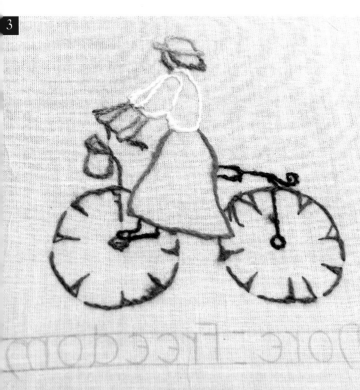

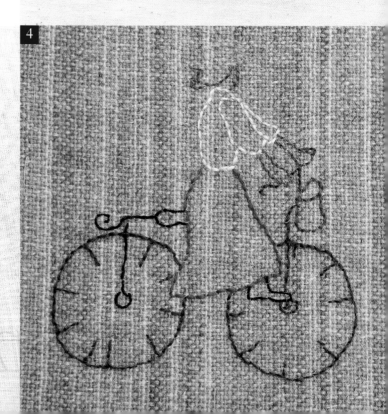

Transposing the design

To overcome the problem of transposing a complicated design on to a rough woollen fabric, a 'trapunto quilting' technique is used. This is a most unusual, yet successful, way of transferring an embroidery design.

1. The 'cartoon' or design.

2. The calico fabric showing the blue transfer pencil and a slight burn mark from the iron! (do not worry if this happens to yours - this is the back).

3. The calico side (back of work) with the outline stitching completed showing all the knots and fastenings off.

4. The woollen fabric (front of work) with the outline completed using the correct colours of wool. Within the kit instructions you will find details of which colours of 'Appleton's Wools' to use and where to use them. After finishing the outline, turn the fabric over in the hoop so that the woollen cloth is uppermost.

In the following photographs, showing the step-by-step stitch techniques, I have used a red colour of thread to show all the six stitches used in the Quaker Tapestry technique.

The dark colours of wool do not show the details sufficiently for demonstration purposes.

Stem stitch outline

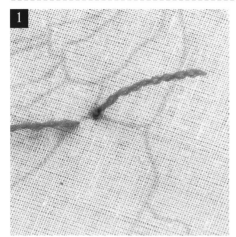

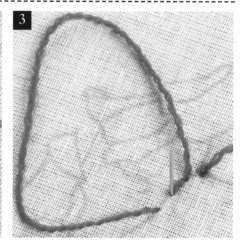

1. Go down with your needle into the calico cloth on the blue transferred line. Pull the thread underneath until the knot sits on top of the calico. Bring the needle back from the underside through the fabric, a stitch away from the knot.

All the knots and finishing-off with your thread should appear on the calico side of your work.

2. Working towards yourself, go down with your needle, a stitch away from the gap. Then come back up with your needle to the start of that stitch - this creates a starter stitch.

Don't worry about the gap on the calico side - the stitch is where you need it on the woollen side.

3. Holding your lead thread to the left (as in photo 2). Go down with your needle to make another stitch towards you - keep hold of the lead thread until you bring your needle back to the top of your work at the end of the starter stitch. Then let go the lead thread and pull the stitch taut - but not too tight.

Remember the stitching technique
- it is really important to use the stab method with your needle because you are using two pieces of fabric together
- always keep your needle straight as you sew.

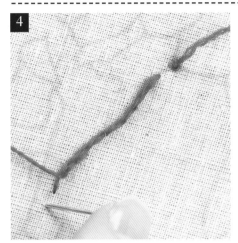

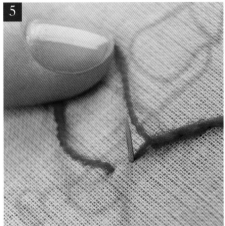

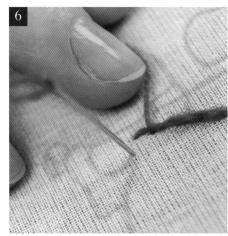

4. Continue with the stem stitch in this way, making a long stitch towards yourself and down, and a short stitch back up to the end of the last stitch, until you begin to run out of thread.

How to sew a corner in stem stitch outline

5. Go down into the corner with your needle and back up to the end of the last stitch as usual.

6. Then put your needle into the blue design line a stitch away from the corner... *continues on next page*.

7. Then come back up with your needle into the corner. Continue sewing the outline until your thread is too short.

10. Then cut off the surplus thread.

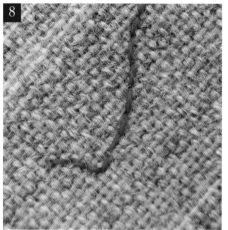

8. Woollen side of work showing the reverse of the stem stitch and completed corner. This neat line of connected stitches on the woollen side forms the outline you will need to infill later. This line of stitches can also be whipped (see page 26) as in the spokes of the wheels and the woman's arms and face.

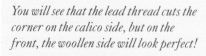

You will see that the lead thread cuts the corner on the calico side, but on the front, the woollen side will look perfect!

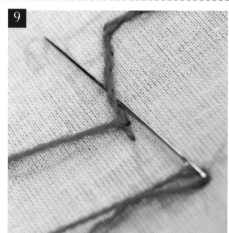

Finishing off the thread at the calico side

9. With your needle still at the calico side, weave the needle through some of the stitches a few times, without going into the fabric

Remember - to use a starter stitch when you start a new piece of thread (see page 20, step 1, 2 and 3).

Complete the rest of the
outline in this way, using the
correct colours of thread.

more freedom

Where to begin the embroidery?

Order of work... If you are creating a design with a background image like the house featured in the gardener kit, then this is where you would begin. This helps to give a 3-dimensional effect and create perspective.

The woman is sitting on top of the bike so in this case, the bike is in the background and this is where we begin to embroider.

Order of embroidery for the 'More Freedom' sewing kit

Here, I suggest an order of work for the embroidery:

1. Spokes of the wheels - whipping stitch (p.26)
2. Wheel tyres - chain stitch (p.28)
3. Arms & face - whipping stitch (p.26)
4. Bike seat - split stitch (p.32)
5. Bike frame - Quaker stitch (two threads) (p.36)
6. Woman's boot - stem stitch (p.34)
7. Woman's skirt - Bayeux point (p.40)
8. Woman's left shirt sleeve (the one at the back) - Bayeux point foundation layer only (p.40)
9. Woman's shirt - Bayeux point (p.40)
10. Woman's right shirt sleeve - Bayeux point foundation layer only (p.40)
11. Woman's hair - chain stitch (p.28)
12. Woman's hat - stem stitch (p.34)
13. Hat band - Quaker stitch (one thread) (p.36)
14. Bike basket - chain stitch (p.28)
15. Lettering - Quaker stitch (one thread) (p.46)
16. don't forget her nose - Peking knot (p.44)

Whipping stitch

Whipping means to coil a thread around another stitch to make it thicker. There are many crewel embroidery stitches that can be whipped to add colour and texture.

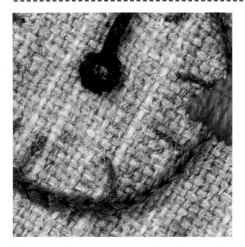

Used to whip the spokes of the wheels and the arms and face, to help create a more definite line.

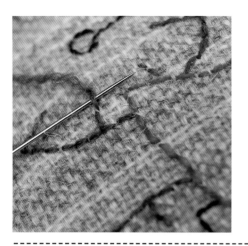

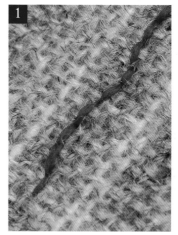

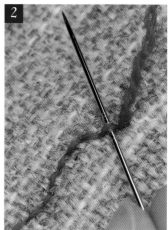

Method of working whipping stitch:

1. This shows the neat little line of connected straight stitches created by the stem stich outline (see page 22). Using the same colour of thread, with a knot at the end, come up with your needle at the beginning of the line of stitching you are whipping. (Remember the knots stay on the calico side).

2. Pass the needle through each stitch, without piercing the woollen fabric.

Other examples of the Whipping stitch:
• Gardener kit (arm)
• Cricketers kit (face and collar)

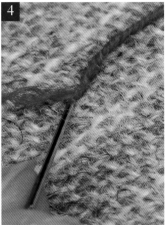

3. After completing a few stitches, pull the thread tight and continue whipping to the end of the row of stitches.

4. Finish by taking the needle down to the back (calico side) and weave into the back of a few stitches to hold the thread secure before you continue to whip the other spokes or to change your thread.

Chain stitch

One of the oldest and most versatile stitches, it forms an interlocking flat chain and can be adapted for a large number of variations.

Used to embroider the wheels and the basket on the bike.

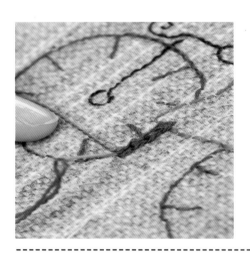

Method of working chain stitch:

Begin by bringing the needle up from the back.

1. Go back down with your needle into the same hole - but make sure you leave a large loop of thread on top of the woollen fabric.

2. Come up with your needle, inside the loop, where you would like the stitch to end (the length of the stitch)

3. Pull the thread gently towards yourself to make the first chain stitch.

Tip - Do not pull this stitch too tight. Let the loop sit on top of the fabric.

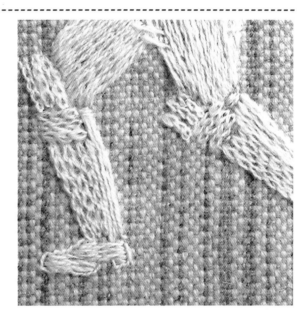

4. Repeat this stitch, always putting the needle in where the thread came out, inside the previous loop. When you run out of thread or you finish the line of stitching, make a little 'couching stitch' at the end by taking the needle down, just outside the loop. This will hold the stitch in place.

5. Completed stitch.

Variation on the Chain stitch:
Detached Chain stitch

The detached chain stitch is also known as the Lazy Daisy Stitch because of its petal-like nature.

The Sheep & Dog kit. Different lengths of detached chain stitch have been used on the sheep's fleece.

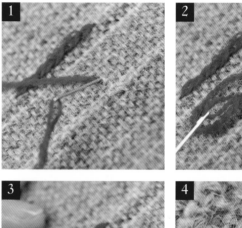

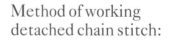

Method of working detached chain stitch:

1. Bring the needle up from the back and go back down with your needle into the same hole -but make sure you leave a large loop of thread on top of the woollen fabric.

2. Come up with your needle, inside the loop, where you would like the stitch to finish.

3. Pull the thread gently to make the first chain stitch.

4. Make a little 'couching stitch' at the end by taking the needle down, just outside the loop. This will secure the stitch.

Variation on the Chain stitch:
Open Chain stitch or Fly stitch

This variation of the chain stitch is used widely in the Quaker Tapestry.

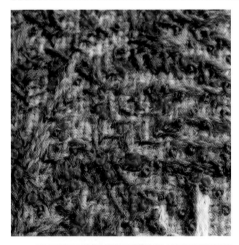

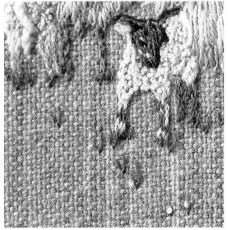

The Gardener kit. The open chain stitch is used on the tree leaves.

The Sheep & Dog kit. The open chain stitch is used for the grass.

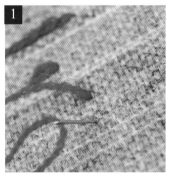

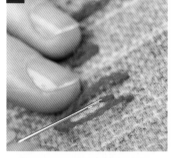

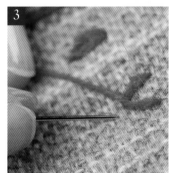

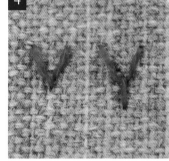

Method of working open chain stitch:

1. Bring the needle up from the back and take the needle down a short distance away from the starting point. Make sure you leave a large loop of thread on top of the woollen fabric.

2. Come up with your needle, inside the loop, where you would like the stitch to finish.

3. Pull the thread gently to form a V shape.

4. Make a little 'couching stitch' by taking the needle down, just outside the point, at the bottom of the stitch (a variation on this could be a longer couching stitch).

Split stitch

Split stitch creates one of the finest lines in embroidery and is therefore useful for fine detail.

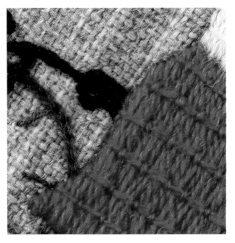

Used to sew the bike seat.

Method of working split stitch:

1. Bring your needle up from the back and make one stitch.

2. As you come up again with your needle, split the stitch, you have just made, in half.

When using this stitch I always like to begin sewing in the middle of the shape to be filled in.

Tip - if you were stitching a large shape with a long row of stitching - at the back of your work, weave the lead thread into a few stitches, working back towards the beginning before starting the next row. This avoids long loops of thread on the back (calico side).

Other examples of the Split stitch:
- Sheep & Dog kit (sheep and dogs face)
- Gardener kit (waistcoat back)

3. Continue stitching in this way until the row of stitching is finished.

4. On the last stitch, go into the end of the last stitch to finish off.

5. Before starting the next row of stitching, go back underneath to where you started from and begin the next row of stitching as before, alongside the first row, until the shape has been filled in.

Stem Stitch

Stem stitch is a very ancient stitch, used in basket making before embroidery was invented. It was found in crewel embroidery from the fifth century and is therefore sometimes known as crewel stitch. It can be used as infill or as a single line.

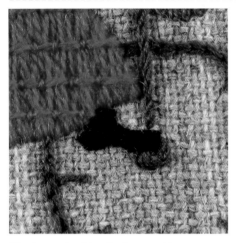

Used to embroider the boot and hat.
Begin with the boot.

When using this stitch I always like to begin sewing in the middle of the shape to be filled in.

Method of working stem stitch:

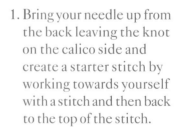

1. Bring your needle up from the back leaving the knot on the calico side and create a starter stitch by working towards yourself with a stitch and then back to the top of the stitch.

2. The next stitch will seem quite long because it is twice as long as the starter stitch. Keep hold of the lead thread as you come back to the surface of the fabric with your needle at the end of the starter stitch.

3. Let go the lead thread and pull the stitch taut but not tight. Continue stitching in this way making a long stitch forward and a short stitch back to the end of the previous stitch.

Other examples of the Stem stitch infill:
• Sheep & Dog kit (dogs coat)
• Gardener kit (shirt sleeve)

4. The last stitch in the row will be a short one to neaten the end - go down with your needle into the end of the last stitch.

5. You can now take your needle back to the start of the shape you are infilling to begin another row. If the shape is large, at the back of your work (calico side), weave the lead thread into a few stitches, working back towards the beginning before starting the next row.

Begin the next row of stitching in the same way, using a starter stitch at the beginning. Complete the shape.

Quaker stitch

The founder of the Quaker Tapestry, Anne Wynn-Wilson, created the Quaker stitch. It is worked using a combination of the stem stitch and the split stitch, which forms a cord or rope-like stitch.

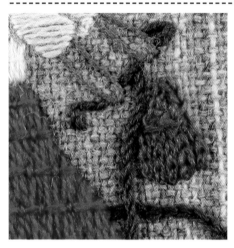

Used to sew the bike frame and handlebars, the hatband and the lettering.

Method of working Quaker stitch using two threads (as in the bike frame):

Cut a long length of thread, (double the usual length) measuring from your little finger to your elbow twice, and thread your needle.

1. Bring the two ends of your thread together and form a knot. Bring your needle up from the back leaving the large knot on the calico side.

2. Make one starter stitch by going down with the needle to make a stitch...

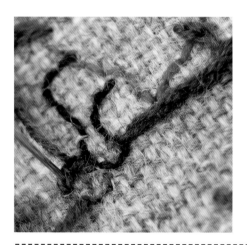

Worked with one thread, it produces a fine flexible line with no stray ends and is therefore very good for the lettering. It can also be sewn using two or four threads together to create larger cords or lines of stitching.

3. ...then back up again at the top of the stitch (avoiding the large knot).

4. Then, because we are using more than one thread, we need to twist the threads together to create the cord. To do this, hold the needle between your fingers and thumb and twist the needle clockwise.

Remember
- if you are working with one thread of wool, do not add the twist- there is no need.

5. With practise, you will get used to how much twisting you need to make the cord. A good tip is to twist the two threads together until they look as if they are one thread. When you loosen your hold it starts to double back to form a rope.

6. Begin the first stitch in the same way you would for the stem stitch by holding your lead thread to the left and working a stitch towards yourself. Take the needle through to the back of the work and keep hold of the lead thread on top.

Other example of the Quaker stitch:
• The cloak worn by Mary Hughes in panel E9
  (embellished area of work which includes the
  Quaker stitch)

7. Bring the needle up through the middle of the starter stitch to split that stitch in half.

8. Now you can let go of the lead thread as you gently pull the thread through to the front of your work - but don't pull too tight - let the stitch sit proudly on the surface of the fabric.

9. Sew a few more stitches and you will see that the cord or rope will start to form.

10. When finishing a row of stitches, go into the end of the last stitch, as you did with the other stitches.

Important -
on a curved line, work in
an anti-clockwise direction,
always throwing the lead
thread to the outside of
the curve.

Left-handed workers may
find it easier to work this
stitch away from themselves,
still working anti-clockwise,
but throwing the lead thread
to the right

Bayeux point

This method of laying threads has gained its name from the 11th century Bayeux Tapestry. In Bayeux point the majority of the wool remains on the surface, so it is a very economical and suitable technique for decorative work.

Used to embroider the skirt and shirt. Begin with the red skirt.

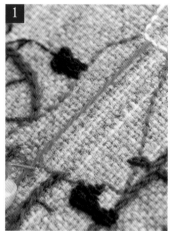

Method of working Bayeux point:

Step one - the *foundation layer* (long in-fill stitches from top to the bottom of a shape):

Using a slightly longer length of thread, begin in the centre of the shape and come up with your needle at the top (at the woman's waist)

1. Lay the thread over the shape, and using the vertical lines of the woollen cloth to guide you, go down with your needle at the bottom of the shape (don't pull these stitches too tight or the background fabric will distort)

2. Come back up with your needle at the bottom of the shape, leaving at least the width of one thread between each stitch.

3. Then go down with your needle at the top (most of the wool will be on the surface of the fabric and not on the calico side).

4. Continue stitching to the edge of the shape.

5. Then go back the other way filling in the gaps as you sew until the shape is a solid colour and you cannot see the background fabric through the stitches.

There are examples on the Quaker Tapestry of quite complex embellished Bayeux point, where the step two and three stages of Bayeux are replaced with other stitches to hold the fabric in place. You can also use just the step one, foundation layer by itself if the shape to infill is small.

Clockwise from top left:
Detail from panel E2 John Bellers (Queen's dress)
Detail from panel D2 Simplicity (Queen's dress)
Detail from panel B1 Firbank Fell (George Fox's hair)
Detail from panel E9 Mary Hughes (Cloak)

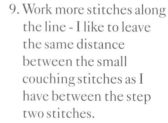
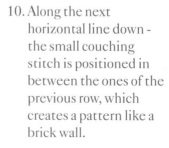

Step two - the *couching layer* (long couching stitches the full width of the shape):

6. This is done in a similar way to step one but leaving a larger gap between the long stitches. The distance between the rows depends on what sort of look you want when it is finished.

Step three - the *couching layer* (small couching stitches securing the long couching stitches):

7. The small couching stitches are worked along the long couching stitch of step two. Come up with your needle, through the foundation stitches, at one side of the long couching stitch horizontal line.

8. Go down at the other side of the horizontal line.

9. Work more stitches along the line - I like to leave the same distance between the small couching stitches as I have between the step two stitches.

10. Along the next horizontal line down - the small couching stitch is positioned in between the ones of the previous row, which creates a pattern like a brick wall.

Top tip - always split one of the foundation layer threads as you create the small couching stitches so that the foundation stitches do not become divided.

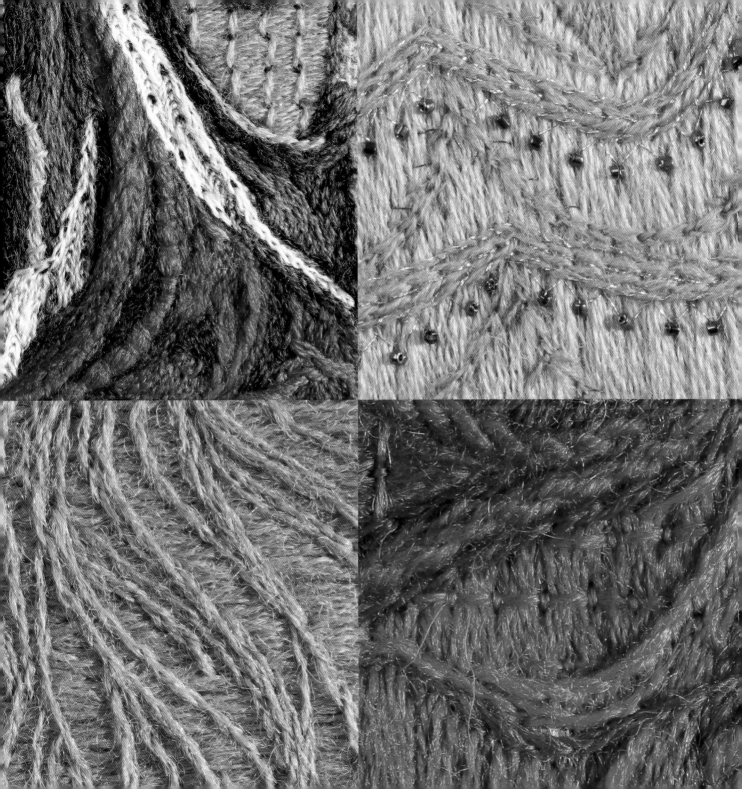

Knot stitch or Peking Knot

As used in Chinese Embroidery, Knot stitch is versatile. It may be used as a seeded filling or a rough knobbly texture. Single knots can represent a full stop, a button or fine lace, or be used as solid filling for curly hair or flowers.

Used to sew the woman's nose.

Below: The Sheep & Dog kit. The Peking knot is shown on the sheep's head, and the lamb's body.

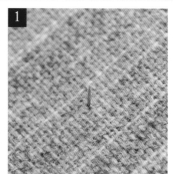

Method of working Knot stitch:

1. Bring the needle up from the back of the fabric.
2. Hold the lead thread in your left hand.
3. Wind it around the needle once.
4. Take the needle down to the surface of the fabric, put the needle into the woollen fabric close to where the thread came out.

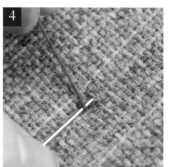

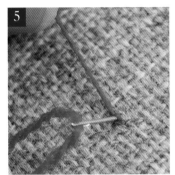

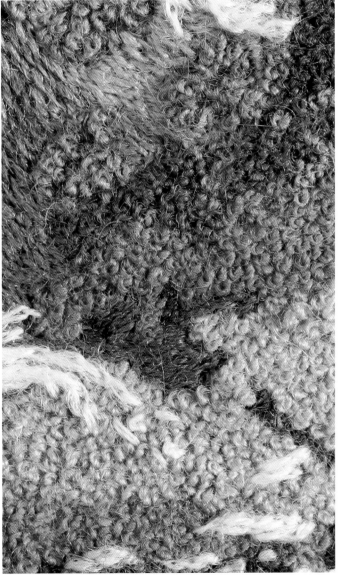

5. Keep the lead thread taut in your left hand while you push the needle down into the fabric with your right.

6. Don't let go of the lead thread until the last moment.

7. Don't pull the knot too tight - leave the little knot sitting on top of the fabric.

Embroidered lowercase lettering using the 'Quaker Stitch'

The lowercase letters are constructed directly on to the front of the fabric in Quaker stitch using one thread.

Always sew letters from the woollen side - you can't rush this; just work one letter at a time.

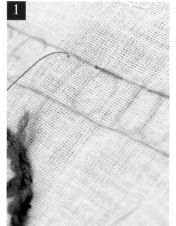

More Freedom sewing kit

1. From the calico side, using a bright cotton sewing thread, carefully sew a row of tacking stitches along the pencil guidelines above and below the letters.

2. Keep your stitches straight - these lines will help guide your embroidery later.

3. Let's start with the letter 'e' using pins, push one pin through the top centre of the 'e'. Push another pin through the bottom centre.

  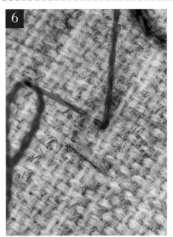 

4. On the woollen side, using the aqua pen provided in your kit, make little dots with the pen where the pins come through.

5. Keep moving the pins around the letter and making dots with the aqua pen until you have a 'dot-to-dot' you can join to draw the letter 'e' in the Quaker Tapestry style.

Progression of embroidery

6. When you are happy with a letter, sew it using the Quaker stitch with <u>one thread</u>. (see Quaker stitch on pages 36, 37 & 38)

7. When you have finished all the lettering, remove any traces of the aqua pen with a barely damp tissue. The bright cotton thread can be pulled out when the lettering is finished.

Test your letter by pushing a pin through the start of the letter from the woollen side and seeing if it emerges in the correct place on the calico side. If not you can use a barely damp tissue to remove the aqua pen mark and start again when the area is dry.

Remember - when working with one thread of wool, do not add the twist - there is no need.

Important - on a curved line, work in an anti-clockwise direction, always throwing the lead thread to the outside of the curve

Embroidered uppercase lettering using the 'Quaker Stitch'

The UPPERCASE LETTERS are quite simple to embroider; they are drawn on to the fabric in the same way as the rest of the design, using the transfer pencil.

1. The outline is worked from the back in stem stitch revealing the running stitch on the woollen fabric to infill with Quaker stitch.

2. The letters are completed on the front of the fabric using Quaker stitch with 4 threads.

3. If the letter is very large the Quaker stitch may be outlined with fine chain stitch, this will give a sculptured look to the finished letter.

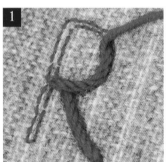

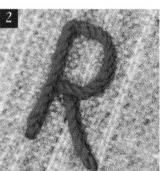

Creating your own designs with lowercase lettering

Where lettering is included in the Quaker Tapestry sewing kit, the layout has been completed for you.

When designing your own lettering for embroidery, I suggest you practise drawing the letters using 5mm squared paper and an ordinary pencil.

The design of the lettering is based on 5mm squared paper as shown in the diagram (page 50 and 51).

When you are ready to put letters together to form words, the space between each letter will vary according to the letters used. A good guide is to have about 1½ squares (7-8mm) between straight letters and one square (5mm) between curved letters. You will notice that the distance between the letters looks rather large when in pencil on paper but remember, the embroidery wool will fatten out the letters and fill the space.

The space between words is about 3 to 4 squares (15-20mm).

As you create the design, on paper, your eyes will be the judge of whether the distances between the letters and words are correct or need some adjustment. Getting it right on paper will save a lot of unnecessary heartache later and your finished embroidery will look wonderful too!

A detail from panel A2 James Nayler.

Quaker Tapestry alphabet

The lowercase alphabet was designed originally by Anne Wynn-Wilson. Small samplers or design are best suited to the lowercase lettering.

The uppercase alphabet was designed by Joe McCrum, an industrial designer and artist, who also worked on the design of 19 Quaker Tapestry panels.

The uppercase letters can be reduced or enlarged with the use of a photocopier to suit the design you're working on. The size shown here is the average size used for titles on the Quaker Tapestry panels.

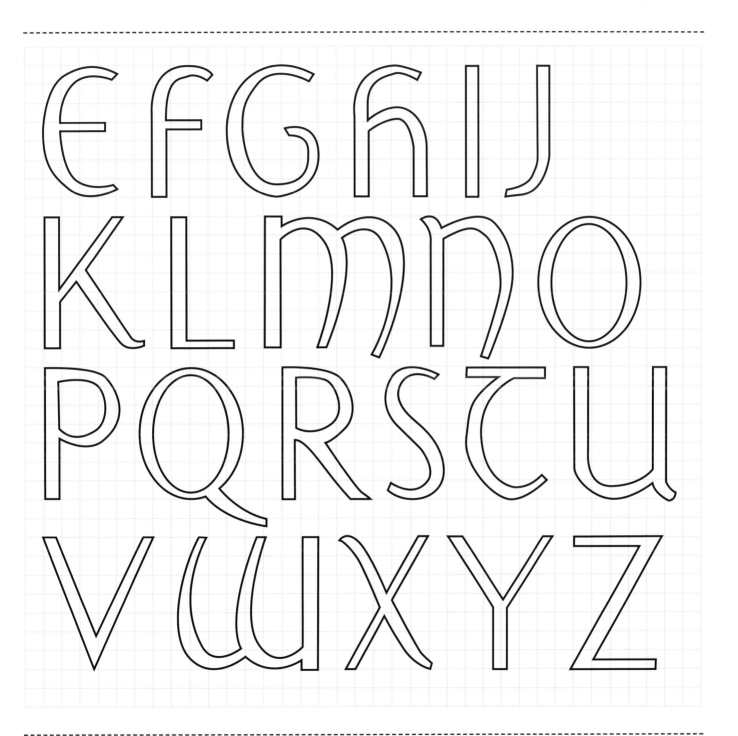

Embellishment of the More Freedom kit

This is a popular embroidery workshop kit, possibly because the lady on the bike was designed and embroidered by a child and not only is it delightful, it's a nice simple design to begin with.

The design can also be adapted to include more embroidery. I have seen many creative variations of this kit with additions of a little dog chasing the bike, a larger basket complete with newspaper and French loaf and background details such as houses and trees etc.

The two embellished designs shown here were embroidered by one of my students, Madeleine Maddox who very kindly allowed me to feature them in this book.

Why not try making it unique by experimenting with your own ideas.

Quaker Tapestry publications

Books:

'Pictorial Guide to the Quaker Tapestry' by Edward H. Milligan (1996)
ISBN: 0-9525433-1-1

'Living Threads the making of the Quaker Tapestry' by Jennie Levin (1999)
ISBN: 0-9525433-3-8

'The Golden Age of Quaker Botanists' by Ann Nichols (2006)
ISBN: 0-9525433-7-0

'The Quaker Tapestry, an introductory guide' (2009)
ISBN: 978-0-9558646-0-5

Films:

'The Quaker Tapestry, an introduction to the project, the embroidery technique and the stitches' - an embroidery workshop film. Written, produced and presented by Bridget Guest (2005)
ISBN: 0-9525433-6-2

'George Fox and the history of the early Quakers' - a short film. Written by Julian Abraham, produced and directed by Bridget Guest.
ISBN: 0-9525433-8-9

Embroidery kits featured in this publication:

- More Freedom
- Sheep & Dog
- Gardener
- Cricketers

See the website shop for more sewing kits or request a mail order catalogue. Phone: 01539 722975.

Quaker Tapestry panel reproductions
©Quaker Tapestry Scheme

Produced by
The Quaker Tapestry at Kendal © 2010

ISBN: 978-0-9558646-1-2

Photographs by Lucy Barden Photography, designed by Cactus Creative and printed by Shanleys Ltd.

For more information about the Quaker Tapestry visit the website:
www.quaker-tapestry.co.uk